D1561690

Sexy Games for Couples

Allison Eden

Copyright © 2022 by Words Are Swords Publishing. All rights reserved.

Published in the United States of America by Words Are Swords Publishing, Los Angeles, CA.

www.WordsAreSwordsPublishing.com

No part of this book may be reproduced, stored in any retrieval system, or transmitted by any means, electronic, scanned, photocopied, or otherwise, without prior written permission of the author or publisher, with the exception of brief passages used for review.

Sexy Games for Couples

2022 EDITION

Written by Allison Eden.

First Edition.

Sexy, Dirty, Naughty Games for Couples

2022 Edition

The 2022 Edition of Sexy, Dirty, Naughty Games for Couples includes:

- **Sexual psychology & how playing sex games can benefit relationships**
- **Additional sexy games offers something for every couple ranging from "Vanilla" to "Sex Fiend"**
- **Complete list of Kinks & Fetishes (which do you have?)**
- **Over 100 wilder, wetter & more kinky games than ever before!**
- **Try new things, bond with your partner & fall in love all over again through these sexy games!**

Dedication

This book is dedicated to all of the plain Janes and mundane Marvins who, deep down, have a dirty, nasty, freaky animal that has been waiting for the day it has the opportunity to show itself.

That day is has come at last.

And soon, so will you.

Contents

An Important Message from the Author

I poured my heart, soul, and various bodily fluids into the making of this book. Before we get into the meat and potatoes of these truly titillating games, I have one simple request: Please do not forget to leave a review for this book at some point. The value of book reviews – even just a single review consisting of a few words – can have a tremendous impact on the trajectory of a book, its readers, and the author.

Better yet, if you could spend the next 30 seconds leaving a review for this book within the marketplace you purchased it, it will not only help out *moi*, but it will also help kinky couples across the globe who are searching for new ways to get their freak on, and who are you to deprive them of that?

I am grateful you have chosen to purchase this book and are taking the time to read it. Thank you, and please take a sec to post a review here.

\- Allison Eden

Introduction by Allison Eden

Thank you for reading the 2022 Edition of *Sexy Games for Couples*. My husband and I wrote this book together over the course of 5 years based on our personal experiences. In that time, however, it's undergone many revisions, so there are just a few things I want to point out while you and your spouse are going through this book together on the journey to either improve your sex life, strengthen your relationship, or just have a little fun with someone you love.

1. There were *many* sex games that didn't quite make it into this book because they were either incomplete (*ie, we couldn't work out the rules*), too kinky (*we are into some seriously weird stuff and would honestly feel awkward putting certain things into this book, but maybe one day*) or they just weren't fun enough to want to play a second time. So, what you're about to read are the best sex games in our repertoire.

2. We originally wrote this book to help newlyweds and recently married couples navigate through their honeymoon phase and create an abundant sex life going into married life. I can't stress enough how important it is for newly married couples to not just have lots of sexy, but actually enjoy the sex you have by trying new and interesting things.

3. The book was re-written for the 2022 edition to help not just married couples, but *any* couples of *any* sexual orientation who want to improve their sex life and strengthen their relationship.

There you have it. I hope that couples who are not married will keep an open mind and not be turned off from this book and are still able to implement the many creative sex games within to strengthen their relationship, or at the very least, just have some kinky fun ;-)

- *Allison Eden*

The Benefits of Sex Games

Married Couples

You and your spouse are entering into a brave new world of lifelong commitment with one another. The two of you will share many things while walking down this road of life – love, laughter, fun and finances - but mostly you will be sharing orgasms.

Whether you're looking to spice up your love live or take you passion to the next level, you'll find that the bedroom games provided here in this book are perfect for any man and wife with an open mind and libido. With these sex games for couples, you'll be able to keep your partner pleasantly surprised in the bedroom and for the rest of your lives.

Sex with your spouse should never become tired, repetitive, or boring. As a general guideline to prevent even the most exciting and spicy of games that you both enjoy from becoming dull, never play the same game twice in one month. Instead, talk with your spouse afterwards and see if this is something you both enjoyed and want to keep to play again later on, in a few weeks, or if the two of you would rather move on to play different games with one another.

The most important thing to remember when exploring new sex games together as couples is that the two of you keep an open mind. Creativity and imagination, in addition to proper communication and empathy for your spouse, are all elements that will ensure that there is never a dull moment when you two are alone together in the bedroom. That being said, if you do not feel comfortable doing something, it is equally important that you speak up and tell your partner immediately.

Especially during this period immediately after the two of you are married, you should always be on the lookout for new things that you would like to incorporate into the bedroom. Be expressive with your spouse about new things that you would like to try and why you want to try them. More often than naught, your spouse with be receptive to introducing new elements into the bedroom.

Remember to set firm boundaries with your spouse so no one gets hurt – either emotionally or physically!

Exploring Kinks, Fetishes and "The Weird Stuff"

Kink is anything that veers away from the "normal" or expected sexual path. It's used to describe "things that are of particular sexual curiosity and interest to someone, particularly those things, behaviors, or practices that are outside of normative sexual behavior," explains Kyle Zrenchik, Ph.D., LMFT, ACS, a couples' sex therapist in Minneapolis. The term comes from the Dutch word "kink" referring to a twist or bend in a rope, he adds.

Importantly, kink can be experienced through the realm of fantasy, he adds. One does not have to physically enact their desire in order to derive satisfaction from their kink.

"Kink is something that one may or may not include in their sexual behavior as a way to enhance pleasure and subjective experience. A fetish is something that primarily defines and is inextricably linked to one's sexual behavior," says Zrenchik.

A fetish is typically concentrated on an object or a body part, i.e., latex, leather, or feet, whereas a kink could be an action, sex act, behavior, or even dynamic between partners. Fetishes are often all-encompassing and the focal point of a person's erotic life. A person with a foot fetish, for instance, would not just derive extra pleasure from touching, licking, or seeing feet during sex; instead, they may only want to interact sexually with feet to the exclusion of other things. "They may not engage in any penetrative act at all but will still draw sexual gratification from the act [of interacting with feet]," says Zrenchik.

Outside of sex, the word "fetish" is also used to describe a type of object that's conferred magical powers, and that's how you can think of it in reference to sex. Some people have objects or body parts that are sexually enticing to them and hold power over them in a way that is out of "the ordinary."

Sex therapist Aliyah Moore, Ph.D., says you can differentiate between the two using this simple quiz:

1. Am I aroused by a thing or an action?
2. Do I need it to be present to be aroused?
3. Can I enjoy solo sex without it being present?

If the answer to item 2 is yes and item 3 no, then you have a fetish. On the other hand, if you answered no and yes for items 2 and 3, respectively, then you have a kink," she says.

Find Your Kink

I realized almost as soon as I put this list together that it would inevitably piss some people the hell off. To any kink aficionados who might be reading this, I just want to apologize ahead of time.

Full disclosure: There is a *lot* more substance behind each of the kinks listed below than I can go into. But since I didn't have time to go deep with each individual kink (phrasing), I will give a brief description followed by a guide for couples who want to experiment and ease themselves into each kink slowly.

Another reason I chose these specific kinks to include in this book is that I have had first-hand experience with each of them as the partner of someone who anxiously admitted their respective kink.

Every partner of mine who told me about their kinks did so with great trepidation. Conversations I've had with people within the kink community all echoed the same thing: *It's common for people who get turned on by something that isn't traditionally accepted as "normal" to experience difficulty communicating it to their partner.* We all have that fear of rejection at certain thresholds, and nothing is scarier than your lover looking at you like you're some kind of freak.

Think about this: When you tell someone you've already had sex with that there is a way for sex between the two (3, 4, or more, no judgments) of you to be even better, which of the following scenarios is most likely to happen?

1. You tell your partner about your kink and they projectile vomit into your mouth and eyes.
2. You tell your partner about your kink and they laugh nervously. R.I.P. eye contact from that point on.
3. You tell your partner about your kink and they simply walk away, never to be heard from again.
4. You tell your partner about your kink and they begin to grin ear to ear because it also happens to be their secret kink and/or they secretly always wanted to try the same thing.

The Answer: Statistically, scenario #4 is most likely to occur. What are the odds! (Actually, they're very good odds.)

If any of the other scenarios were to occur, it would mean that your partner doesn't trust you and you're just not sexually compatible. Don't take it personally – that's what dating is for, right? To see if you're *compatible.*

Compatibility is everything – **especially sexual compatibility.** After all, you can't force a square peg in a round hole and you can't peg a square their round hole (<u>Translation:</u> if you're adventurous in the bedroom, you need to find a partner who is also adventurous).

You're going to have to trust me on this one: If there is one specific thing that really does it for you - something that gets your loins frothing almost immediately and without fail - but, for whatever reason, you feel ashamed by it - you need to tell your partner!

Maybe not immediately, but as soon as you catch feelings for someone (or visa versa), then it's time to air out your kinks.

I have an unwavering set of rules and boundaries for myself when it comes to the bedroom, and most of them are about communication.

Here is Allison Eden's Rule of When to Tell a New Partner About the Freaky Shit You're Into:

In between fuck session #2 and fuck session #3. Immediately after the second time you bang is always best because there is something to be said about post-coital openness and acceptance.

Alternatively, maybe you've been in a monogamous relationship for years and just want to try something different and exciting. That's fine, too, and you should communicate this need to your partner as soon as possible.

Just tell them the shit you're into, what makes your dick hard, and the things you want to do to your partner – and do it as early as possible! Because the longer you wait, the weirder it will be.

Many people turn their kink into a lifestyle, and for some, it's an identity. Rest assured that there are large communities of underground kinksters for everyone who has a "thing" – and all of them are very welcoming to newcomers.

Surrounding yourself with people who understand and share your "thing" is the best way to stop feeling ashamed by it, enjoy better and more fulfilling sex, and be overall happier and less stressed out in life.

The surprising thing about kinks is that people often don't know what they like until it's right in front of them, and from that point on, it's all they crave.

Even if your partner's kink does absolutely nothing for you, it can be a huge turn on just to see how much they enjoy it, so always keep an open mind and keep the doors of communication open.

Lastly, to everyone else with a specific kink that was not listed in this book, I'm so sorry! Unlike most books about kinks and fetishes, I just didn't feel comfortable writing about something I have no first-hand experience in. You're welcome to punish me as you see fit.

I would love nothing more than to include a more diverse range of kinks, fetishes, positions, and sex games in the next edition of this book. If you have one of these that you would like to see added to this book next year, I encourage you to email me a description of your specific kink, fetish, sex position, or sex game along with any relevant resources or community websites for research. (Dick pics will be filed by skin tone and archived under "Future Extortion Victims")

XOXO, Allison.

- Allison@wordsareswordspublishing.com

BDSM

BDSM is an umbrella term for bondage, discipline/domination, submission/sadism, and masochism. These kinks all hinge on power play—that is, the erotic and voluntary exchange of power. BDSM is all about one party exerting dominance over the other in a mutually consensual, pre-agreed-upon and satisfying encounter. This kink is for you if you fantasize about letting your partner have their way with you, or if you derive pleasure from the idea of "making" your partner service and please you.

Sadism and masochism

Sadism and masochism come under the BDSM umbrella. These kinks are all about your relationship to pain. A sadist derives pleasure from inflicting pain on a sexual partner, and a masochist derives pleasure from receiving it. What do you fantasize about when you masturbate? If your fantasies tend to involve the exchange of pain, perhaps you might want to let your inner sadist or masochist out with an equally game partner?

Ropes and Bondage

Having a bondage or ropes kink is one of the most well-known kinks out there. This one's for you if you enjoy the idea of restricting your partner or being restricted. Maybe it makes you feel safe and taken care of? Or desired and subjugated? Or powerful and in control? Exploring this kink necessitates a safe word so that you can easily end the scene if it becomes too much. Have scissors on hand as well so that ropes can be simply and quickly removed.

Hosiery

This kink is marked by an interest in wearing pantyhose or having a partner wear hosiery while engaging in sexual activity. If you find that you often ask your partner to wear hosiery, or you yourself feel a strong urge to wear them during sex and experience more pleasure when wearing or seeing hosiery, you may have a pantyhose fetish or kink. Explore by buying hosiery, especially kinds made for having sex (i.e., crotchless).

Voyeurism

A voyeurism kink centers on being turned on by watching other people having sex. You might figure out that this is your kink by being particularly turned on by seeing yourself have sex in a mirror. In order to explore this kink more, make sure that you engage in a consensual situation such as at a sex club or sex party.

Exhibitionism

Exhibitionism is all about getting turned on by being observed. If you ever fantasize about having sex, masturbating, or getting naked in front of an audience or want someone to watch you, then you might find this kink enjoyable. You might wish to have sex in settings such as sex clubs, or perhaps you just want to leave the curtains open while you have sex in your bedroom. This kink can be a lot of fun, but make sure that what you're doing won't get you arrested for indecent exposure!

Roleplay

This kink is defined by taking on different personas during sex and experiencing intensified pleasure from stepping outside of yourself. For instance, maybe you and your partner play a librarian and a student, or a delivery worker and a housewife. Are you usually shy but really let go and come harder when you don't have to be yourself? Maybe roleplay is your kink.

Dirty talk

To this date I have never met a human being who didn't enjoy a little dirty talk… especially the shy ones!

Dirty talk is exactly what it sounds like: using suggestive or explicit language during sex in order to heighten sensation and excitement. This might be your kink if you're generally verbose and enjoy using words to feel powerful during sex. You'll know if this is your kink or not if you reach orgasm quicker when talking or being talked to.

Urophilia

Also known as piss play, golden showers, or watersports, this kink is for folks who are sexually aroused by urination—either giving or receiving. You can ease into piss play by starting in the shower and seeing how it feels. If you like it, you can invest in some waterproof blankets and get into it! This kink may be more likely to appeal to you if you're also interested in domination or submission.

Nipple play

Some people might have a nipple kink, either because they themselves have very sensitive nipples and love to have them played with or because they are drawn to their partner's nipples. People who in general find themselves drawn to breasts might find they have a nipple kink. Tweak, lick, and bite your partner's nipples or invite them to do so to yours in order to discover if this is the kink for you. And remember, nipple play is for everyone, not just women. (Yes, male nipple play is a thing!)

Humiliation

A humiliation kink is about being put in your place by a partner. Someone with a humiliation kink might, for example, get off on being told that their penis is too small or that they're pathetic or a slut. Humiliation kinks can also be enacted through different kinds of power play such as bootlicking or facials. It's all about the meaning that the people ascribe to certain acts. Often this kink is theorized to be found in people who live in "high-respect, high-power" positions by day and who want to explore the opposite position.

Cuckolding

A cuckolding kink tends to be more common among men, but people of any gender might enjoy this dynamic. Cuckolding is about being turned on by your partner having sex with someone else, either in front of you or away from you and relaying details at a later date. A cuckold is aroused by the idea of sharing their partner and also by the implied humiliation in "not being able to wholly satisfy" them.

Female-led relationships

Female-led relationships (FLR) is all about women on top. People with an FLR kink are turned on by giving the woman in a heterosexual relationship the bulk of the sexual control. This could look like sex centering on her pleasure or her deciding when and how sex should be had. You might have an FLR kink if you're a man who tends toward submission in many areas of life, or if you're a woman who likes the idea of subverting traditional female gender roles.

Financial domination

Financial domination, aka FinDom, is often a fetish but can also be a kink. (All you "Pay Pigs" know what I'm talking about!) It involves giving over total control of one's finances to someone else or being kept on a strict budget or being ordered to purchase certain things. This kink is for you if the idea of giving over so much control in such an important part of life turns you on. You can explore it by beginning with a trusted partner and introducing a financial element into your sex life. For instance, one could say that 10% of your monthly income must be spent on sexy presents for your partner and go from there.

Auralism

Auralism is just the word for having a sound kink, i.e. being turned on by hearing things. For example, you might be extra aroused by hearing the sound of your partner hit against you as you have sex, or the sound of their moans or how wet they are. You can explore this kink by trying to dampen out other senses, by using a blindfold for instance, so you can focus on the noises. If you've ever gotten tingly listening to ASMR or the sound effects in audio erotica, this might be your kink.

Age play

This kink is a specific type of roleplay where one or two consenting adults take on roles or ages other than their own.. This could be your kink if you've ever gotten a flutter from being called baby, little boy/girl, Mummy, or Daddy in bed. Age play can range from using different names to literally dressing up like a baby; it all depends on what you feel comfortable with and turned on by.

Orgasm control

This kink is common among people who are generally interested in BDSM. It's exactly what it says on the tin: letting your partner control the timing of your orgasm. This is often achieved through the use of bondage. The dominant partner restrains the submissive partner and stimulates them to the brink of orgasm—only letting them come when/if the dominant partner wants to. You might be into this kink if you're interested in submitting your pleasure to someone else or if you love giving or getting a ruined orgasm.

Impact play

Impact play is just the fancy name for any activity like spanking, paddling, or caning.

Being hit in a consensual erotic context releases endorphins, which can give participants a real rush, says licensed therapist Ashera DeRosa, LMFT. DeRosa recommends "exploring spanking followed by caresses as a really fun way to explore the sense of touch." This kink speaks to people who like to experiment with power and sensation.

Consensual Nonconsent

Consensual nonconsent is a kink in which someone is turned on by the idea of being "taken" by their partner while they pretend to say no. Sometimes referred to as a "rape fantasy," this kink is always pre-agreed-on and must be carefully negotiated by all parties involved. There is evidence that people who have experienced sexual assault can find this type of scene healing because they get to have some control over it, but there are many people who have not experienced sexual trauma who enjoy it as well.

Gags

Having a gag kink can mean that you're turned on by wearing or making your partner wear a gag of some kind. Ball-gags or silicone bits are common toys to use for this. This kink speaks to people who love the feeling of being at someone's mercy and not being able to speak. It's important when exploring this kink that the person who is gagged can still communicate. Carey suggests that they can hold a little bell in their hand or drop a ball for attention if they need the play to stop.

Praise kink

Someone with a praise kink is aroused by compliments, praise, and encouragement—for instance, being told "You're doing such a good job, taking my cock" or "You're so beautiful when you..." While most people like to receive compliments, someone with a praise kink will be really sent over the edge by receiving them in a sexual setting. People who are a little unsure of themselves or who struggle with attachment issues may be particularly into this kink.

Degradation kink

A degradation kink can be considered the opposite of a praise kink. A person with this kink is turned on by being denigrated and degraded by their partner either through words or through actions (i.e., being spit on). This kink might do something for you if you lean toward being submissive and like your partner to take control and tell you what to do in a sexual situation.

Blood play

Blood play is all about being aroused by blood, either by having your own brought to the surface or drawing your partner's blood. A blood kink might speak to people who are turned on by vampires or those who enjoy inflicting or receiving pain (sadists and masochists). Make sure to use well-sterilized objects to draw blood, have a safe word, and preferably take a class from an experienced domme who can show you how to indulge this kink safely.

Autoplushophilia (furries)

Known in everyday speech as a "furry kink," autoplushophilia "involves dressing up in animal costumes and engaging in sexual play," explains Lawrenz. A furry is someone who is turned on by imagining themselves and others as anthropomorphic animals. As a sexual practice, this is often a very fun way to connect with your partner. If you like to dress up or have a huge stuffed animal collection—this kink may be for you.

Mummification

This kink isn't anything to do with motherhood; instead, it's about mummies in the ancient Egyptian sense. People with a mummification kink get turned on by wrapping their partners tightly in Saran wrap, or being tightly wrapped themselves. After being wrapped up, pictures are sometimes taken for gratification at a later date. Make sure to leave air holes around the nose and mouth, warns Lawrenz. This kink is for you if you're into restraint and control (and ancient history!).

Things to keep in mind when exploring kinks.

Whenever you play around with kinks, especially those that have a BDSM element, it's very important to engage in aftercare. A major rush of endorphins can feel euphoric, but once that ends, many people report feeling a 'drop.' Having a plan to cuddle, have food and water, and/or watch a show that feels familiar and comforting afterward can help round out the experience and feel more connective.

Sexy Games for All Types of Relationships

Whether it is your first-time having sex as a couple or your 1,000th, couples may still have a lot of questions on their minds about what the sex will be like as their relationship evolves.

What will sex be like after you and your spouse move in together? What if we start sharing finances? What if we get married? Have kids? What will our sex life look like 10 or 20 years from now???

While committed, long-term relationships may change many aspects of your life, it will only serve to improve you sex life by inviting more passion into the bedroom than ever before – if you make it a priority!

It's a common misconception that just because you are going to be having sex with the same person for the rest of your life (2-3 years if you live in Hollywood, CA like I do) doesn't mean that sex should ever become boring.

On the contrary – married sex can be some of the most passionate, exciting, and pleasurable sex that you will ever have. The important thing to remember with these sex games for couples is to keep and open mind and to keep communication as open as possible. Especially important right after marriage, make sure that you make time to get to know your lover, what turns them on, things that they like as well as the things that they don't like. Once you know your spouse inside and out you will always be able to keep your sex life fresh and interesting by bringing these sex games for couples into the bedroom.

The important thing to remember when getting to know your spouse's sensual side is that communication is a two-way street. If you find that your love doesn't know how to please you or is doing things that do not turn you on, the best thing you can do is to speak up!

Having an open vein of communication is especially important in the bedroom, just as it is important in very other area of your relationship.

During foreplay or even during the act, let your spouse know what you want from them. Then ask them what they want from you. You'll find that by having open sexual communication, you will soon be enjoying some of the best lovemaking of your entire life, for the rest of your life. This is especially important at the beginning of any relationship that you lay the proper sexual cornerstones for your respective likes and dislikes.

Lastly – and this message applies to both men and women – you MUST find a way to tell your partner what they're doing doesn't feel good and/or could be improved without hurting their feelings. Some couples a very blunt about such things, but usually couples will suffer through years of bad sex before it eventually destroys their sexless relationship.

Communication is key!

Truth or Dare

Do you remember playing truth or dare with your friends when you are a kid? This game is a timeless classic that can easily be adapted into a sex game for couples. If you've never played Truth of Dare, the rules are simple. Ask your lover to choose Truth or Dare. If they choose Truth, ask them a question and they must answer honestly. If they answer Dare, you dare them to do something naughty. If they are unable to complete the Dare, then ask them a naughty question instead.

One of the great things about this classic game is that Truth of Dare can be played through text messages while you are both at work or away from one another. This is another great way to build up sexual tension for the next time you see one another.

Here are a few examples of naughty Truths to get you started:

- What is your favorite part of my body?
- What is your favorite memory of us having sex?

Asking your spouse to answer a Truth is also a brilliant way to gauge their interest in a sexual fantasy that has been on your mind or you have considered trying, such as:

- Would you ever have sex in public?

- Have you ever had a fantasy about BDSM?

The same goes for Dares. Here are some examples to get you started:

- I dare you to use a toy on yourself while I watch.
- I dare you to watch an entire adult film without touching yourself.

Or if you are away from one another or at work:

- I dare you to take a naked selfie in the bathroom and send it to me.
- I dare you to take your underwear off and go the rest of the day without it.

As with any sex game for couples, keep it fun and safe.

Strip Poker / Strip Anything

Strip poker is a classic game that couples and cheeky singles have been playing for generations. If you don't know how to play poker, a "strip" variation can be applied to almost any game. Choose a game that you both know how to play and enjoy. You don't want to end up boring your spouse either with the game itself or by trying to teach them the rules to a new game. This is a great opportunity to have fun with your spouse as you excite and explore one another.

What is your favorite childhood game? Shoots and Ladders? Connect Four? Try Strip Shoots and Ladders and Strip Connect Four. Any time that your spouse scores, wins a hand or moves forward, you must remove an article of clothing and vice versa. Keep playing until one player is completely naked, at which point the other players gets to request one sexual favor from the player who has lost all of their clothes.

The beauty of these Strip-Anything games is that this is a game that you can play with your spouse on a nightly basis with a different game each night and it will still be fun and interesting. Each night there will be a different game, different winner and different sexual favors, which gives this sex game for couples limitless possibilities.

Play nice! No one likes a sore loser.

Get yourself a poker game night set, complete with cards, chips and dice, here: https://amzn.to/34LVxwa

(I've used the same set to host a couples game night, then play a little after hours strip poker)

Also fun: Strip Jenga. Or better yet, Naughty Jenga. (https://amzn.to/3uQVqdI)

Twister

Twister is one of the original games that can be non-sexual when we played at as children, but also has the potential to be a fun sex game for couples.

This is one of the most popular choices when it comes to having plain, unadulterated, and often a sexy good time. The box of this classic game includes a spinner and a plastic mat marked with colored circles. After the dial is spun, players are required to move a hand or foot to the marked circles. As the game progresses, it becomes increasingly necessary to contort one's body into ludicrous poses and herein lies the fun.

Very often even before the end of the game, players succumb to laughter and the limitations of the human body.

For couples, Twister takes on a whole new meaning when this game is played with absolutely no clothes on. For the adult version, have the winner request a sensual favor from his or her opponent.

You can find the original game Twister here: https://amzn.to/34LVxwa

Scavenger Hunt

This classic at kid's parties can be given an adult twist to make it truly enjoyable for couples. This is especially fun when your spouse is out of the house or at work and you are home alone. You can leave clues for your spouse all over the house and let one clue lead to the next, starting from the front door or wherever you know that they will be entering when they get home.

For instance, to indicate that the next clue can be found behind the bathroom mirror, let the previous one read, "I can see my reflection in your eyes", or some similar other hints about mirrors. The hints as romantic or as provocative as possible as well as being linear and relatively simple. You want to excite your spouse and not confuse him or her. You also want the route of your scavenger hunt to lead directly to the bedroom in no more than 3 to 5 hints.

Once your spouse makes it to the bedroom, congratulate him or her for solving the scavenger hunt by either laying naked in a provocative pose on the bed, offering yourself as a reward by wrapping yourself in a giant bow, or engaging your lover in one of his or her favorite fantasies that you know they will enjoy.

Sexy Story Time

This is a great game for couples who are creative. Sexy Story Time is just like when you would tell each other scary stories around the bonfire when you were kids at camp. First turn off all of the lights in the bedroom and get comfortable with your spouse on the bed, of if you have a fireplace, this is the perfect opportunity to use that. It might help to be in various states of undress for this one. Instead of telling each other scary stories, you will be telling each other sexy stories.

You don't have to be the Hemingway of Erotica in order to tell a great sexy story. The best place to start is from your own fantasies or maybe an adult movie you have seen. In fact, Sexy Story Time is the perfect opportunity to broach the subject of a sexual fantasy that you have always had that you want to share with your lover. You can describe your fantasy in great detail, and although it may be happening to a fictional character in your story, you can gauge the interest of your spouse afterwards.

If you're describing a specific fetish that you have and have always wanted to try with your spouse and he or she tells you how turned on they are after you are done telling your story, then you should proceed by suggest you try out something similar with them.

Sexy Story Time is much more than a way to test the water of your fantasies. This sex game for couples allows you to be a bit more liberal with your use of dirty talk, because it is all fiction, after all. This game will also allow couples to show off their imagination and sensual side while exciting each other. After all, creativity is the ultimate aphrodisiac.

Sexy Dice

This is a fun sex game for couples that doesn't require as much creativity. All it requires two pairs of dice. Write down or type up a set of body parts that correspond to one dice, 1 through 6. They can be anything, but here are some examples:

1. Lips
2. Ear
3. Nipple
4. Toes
5. Butt
6. Genitals

Next, write down 6 different sexy actions that correspond to the other dice, 1 through 6. Again, they can be anything you want them to be, but here are a few examples:

Lick

Kiss

Bite

Caress

Suck

Tickle

Keep in mind that these are all just examples. The real fun of this game is creating your own, personalized dice based on what you and your partner enjoy. You can also buy pre-made Sexy Dice similar to these here:

https://amzn.to/33msbE1

(These are also good if you and your partner have a hard time deciding on which positions to do)

With this sex game for couples, the possibilities are limitless because you can come up with any number of different acts and any number of body parts you want. If you really want to get creative, try adding in a third dice with more actions, sexual positions, or whatever you want. Sexy Dice can become a new sex game every night!

Tarzan and Jane

This sex game for couples is a great way for couple to get in touch with their primal side. The goal of this game for girls is to do everything in their power to resist their spouse. Meanwhile, the goal of this game for guys is to do everything in his power to wrestle, pin down his wife and tie her hands or feat to the headboards.

This is one of those sex games that could start out funny at first, then quickly become more sexually aggressive as both of your primal sides come out. By the end of game, you'll both be sweaty, horny, and ready for rough sex.

Even if the two of you both enough things a little rough, be sure and play nice with each other and remember your safe word.

Blindfold Treats

This is a fun game of couples who don't mind getting a little dirty in the bedroom. It requires a blindfold and a dessert that you can spoon feed to your spouse, such as ice cream.

The game is simple – you place the blindfold on your spouse and guide them to sit on the edge of the bed. While blindfolded, your spouse needs to successfully navigate a spoon into the dish of ice cream and into your mouth. For every successful mouthful of ice cream, they get a kiss. For every miss – and this is where the fun comes in – your spouse needs to lick the ice cream off of whatever body part it fell on.

It sounds simple, but you might be surprised where the spoon finds itself.

You can pickup a blindfold here:
https://amzn.to/3LBMqig

(These are also amazing for sleep. Did somebody say "personalized blackout curtains"?)

30 Second Blind Date

This is another fun sex game for couples to play with a blindfold. In addition to a blindfold, you will also need some way to keep time for this game, such as a phone or stopwatch. Place the blindfold on your spouse and set the timer for 30 second. It has to make a sound after 30 seconds, or it can be really easy to lose track of time with this game.

Once the timer starts, you have 30 second to do anything you can to turn on your blindfolded partner and bring them to the point of ecstasy. There are no other rules to the game other than the fact that you are doing everything that you can think of to get your spouse off in just 30 seconds. As soon as the timer chimes and 30 seconds is up, very quickly switch the blindfold, resent the time for another 30 seconds and switch roles. Now your spouse has only 30 second to turn you on and get you off. Keep switching off after every 30 seconds until finally someone climaxes for the win.

For a twist on this game, see how long you can last without being turned on by your spouse. You may find this version a little bit more difficult!

This is a favorite game fore many couples because it gives you very little time to think about what you turns on your partner. You simply have to react and see what works best and what doesn't work, which lets you get to know your partner and what turns them on very quickly. This is also a great game for couples to play if they don't have a lot of time on their hands and want to fit in an exciting quickie.

Hot and Cold

This is another food game with uses a blindfold. This can work for either men or women, although women are usually the ones playing the game and men are usually the ones being blindfolded. Start by having a selection of hot and cold items prepared and stashed away that you will later share with your spouse. Dessert items work best, such as ice cream, champagne, warm honey, and other sweet items with different temperatures and different textures.

Tell your spouse that you have a surprise for them and bring them somewhere private, then remove their clothes. Take a little scoop of the dessert of your choice into your mouth, such as ice cream, and give your partner a big, wet kiss. Next, pour a little bit on their body and then seductively lick it off. Finally, put something in your mouth or on their genitals as you perform oral sex on your spouse.

The variety of different temperatures and textures that your use with this game will really add an element of sexy mystery. When you are all done, or all out of food items, the two of you can take a nice, warm shower together.

The Slippery Sex Game

This is another fun sex game for couples that might get a little messy, so be prepared to either throw down a blanket that you don't much care for or be prepared to do a great deal of laundry.

The first part of this game is for the two of you to get as sweaty or slippery as possible. If you have access to a co-ed steam room or sauna, that is a perfect way to quickly get hot and bothered and sweat in each others company. Alternatively, you can turn on the hot water in your shower while the bathroom fills up with steam, which will effectively create your own steam room. The best part about making your own sauna at home is that towels are not required.

Wait until the steam fills up the room and you can really feel yourself sweating before jumping into bed together. In most saunas with will only take between 10 and 15 minutes, but in your "home steam room" in your bathroom, this could take up to 45 minutes depending on how big your bathroom is. You may be surprised at how arousing it is to have sex while you are slipping and sliding all over one another.

You can also use natural oils, such as coconut oil, in order to achieve a similar desired effect. Either way, this is definitely a sex game that every newlywed should try at least once in their life.

If you're going to use lubricant, I strongly recommend this no-stain water-based one: https://amzn.to/36eQYuW

The Don't-Have-Sex Game

Although it may sound a little counter intuitive, this sex game for couples is actually one of the hottest sex games that the two of you can play together. This game is also a very effective tool for building up attraction with one another to the point where you want to rip each others clothes off. While playing this game, you will have your spouse at the bring of arousal that you never thought possible. Just make sure that you agree to the terms before you start playing.

This game could be played over the course of an evening while relaxing at the house. In this sex game, couples try to do everything in their power to seduce their spouse while not actually initiating sex themselves. This can be done by laying naked next to your spouse or by making suggestive noises while he or she watches. By doing everything in your power to turn the other person on while not actually initiating sex, you are able to build and reinforce a very strong form of attraction and arousal in your partner.

The "loser" is the person who inevitably caves and ends up initiating sex. Just make sure that this game doesn't go on for more than 24 hours, or you will both be losers.

Fantasy Role Play Ideas

In this section, we will talk about fulfilling various role-playing fantasies of your spouse. Every person has his or her own fantasies that they wish would come true. In a loving marriage, you can feel free to share these fantasies with your spouse without fear of any insecurities or jealousies coming up. Talk to your partner about the sexy fantasy that you have in mind. Role playing fantasies are some of the best ways to spice up your love life because the scenario is always new and unique.

Some important things to remember when exploring role playing fantasies with your lover is that, first and foremost, it is a fantasy. Explain that you don't really wish that the other person were a fireman or a police officer or any other role playing in your fantasies and that you love the other person just the way they are. It will take a bit of acting and a lot of commitment, especially when you are just starting out with your first role playing fantasy, but stick with it. There will be a lot of giggling at first and it may seem strange to you, but try to stay in character and play into your spouse's fantasy. For fantasies that are a bit more risqué, you may want to establish a safe word that if things ever get too real, when uttered, the fantasy ends and the role playing stops. Above all, have fun with it and be safe.

Costumes and props are also a huge part of role playing fantasies. Although you can find a variety of costumes and props at most adult novelty and toy stores, the best time to stock up on these is in October, just before Halloween. This will also give the two of you an excuse to try out a bunch of different costumes and experiment with different role playing fantasies.

You may have your very specific fantasy in mind, but here are a few role playing games that you may not have thought of or that you may want to try out with your spouse. Try taking turns switching fantasies with your spouse – one night you get to choose the role playing fantasy and the following night your spouse gets to choose one.

Pro-tip: Role-play is seriously a lot more fun when you use props and costumes. It might feel silly at first, but the costume really help you get into character and make this so much hotter.

Sexy Masseuse

Here is a new take on couples massages. Every thought about getting down and dirty during a massage? Even if you haven't this role playing fantasy has plenty of benefits for both partners. All you need is a towel and some massage oils or lotion. We recommend getting the massage oils that are hot to the touch, because lotion can be cold on your naked body and the heating oils feel oh-so good. You don't really need a professional massage table. You can just lay down on your bed, but be careful not to get those heating massage oils on the sheets. You don't want to wrap yourself in your bed sheets later only to get burnt!

If you want to make this role playing fantasy as real as possible, then you'll want to start from the beginning. Walk toward the bedroom, where your spouse, the massage receptionist, is waiting outside. Tell her that you have an appointment to get a massage and she will show you to the massage room, your bedroom. She will ask you to disrobe and lay face down on the massage table, you bed, then leave the room. Maybe she walking in a moment too early to catch you still in the midst of disrobing – how embarrassing!

You should have the cover pulled comfortably up to your lower back and be laying on your stomach by the time the masseuse returns. The masseuse will begin by putting a small amount of lotion or heating oils on your back and rubbing them in with gently pressure, making small circles up and down your back. Maybe at some point the towel slips off, maybe the masseuse's hands slip a little too far under the towel, but either way the role play fantasy inevitably ends with both of you under the sheets.

Like all role playing fantasies, remember to have fun and be creative. Just be sure that you both get a chance to switch up the roles and massage one another.

For more massage techniques see our guide on giving (and getting) massages under the Sex Tips for Couples section.

Your Favorite Movie

Remember that scene for your favorite movie that always turned you on? Titanic? Ghost? Dirty Dancing??

Now you can reenact it with your spouse and fulfill that scene that you have always fantasized about. Depending on how creative you want to get with this role playing fantasy, you may have to invest heavily in new costume and props, but once you have those, that only means that you can relive this fantasy again and again in new and interesting ways.

First, watch the movie with your spouse together. When the scene that you want to role play with him or her is coming up, point it out and tell your spouse that you want to act it out with them. Chances are, they will be all for it. If this is the scene that you wanted to act out then you will be the director as well as the leading role. Get your costumes and props ready, set the scene, make sure that you spouse knows what he or she is supposed to do and then yell "action!"

You can basically turn any scene from a movie, TV show, or adult film into a role playing game. Just remember that you're not going for an Oscar here and that it is all about having fun.

Stranger at a Bar

Here is an exciting role playing fantasy that you and your spouse can play next time you want to go out on a date night. You both get dressed up nicely and leave to a particular bar at separate times, or maybe you both of you head there after work. The wife sits alone at the bar while the husband comes along and introduces himself while hitting on her.

The couple will act like total strangers at the bar and all through the night, giving them a chance to relive the passion of when they first met. You won't know where your spouse is going to be at the bar, you'll just have to find that special someone and rekindle a passion and attraction in them from square one.

This is a fun role play for both husband and wife because they can get totally immersed in their roles for an entire night, even bringing the fantasy back into the bedroom and into the next day.

Even More Role Plays

Here is my personal list of role-play scenarios I've been workshopping. I hope that one of these sparks a bit of inspiration to come up with some of your own (if not, put on some porn and you'll figure it out).

- The teacher and the bad student
- The frisky construction worker and the lonely housewife
- The horny landlord and the broke tenant
- The peeping tom and the exhibitionist
- The jock and the cheerleader
- The doctor / nurse and the patient
- The dominatrix and the submissive slave
- The safari hunter and the wild animal
- The talent agent and the aspiring starlet
- The vampire and the vampire hunter/huntress

Voyeur Sex Bingo

The spice things up another notch, test the limits of your voyeurism by playing Voyeur Sex Bingo using the card on the following page.

VOYEUR SEX BINGO

OUT-DOORS	SAUNA	ELEVATOR	WINDOWS OPEN	PUBLIC RESTROOM
BALCONY	ROOF-TOP	ALLEY-WAY	ON THE HIGHWAY	SOMEONE ELSE'S HOUSE
ON THE BEACH	MAKE A SEXTAPE (STILL COUNTS!)	FREE 	HOT TUB	IN AN ABANDONED BUILDING
PARKING GARAGE	IN A LIBRARY (SHHH!)	IN A PARK	STADIUM BLEECHERS (SPORTS GAME)	BEHIND A DUMPSTER
SEX PARTY	MOVIE THEATER	ON AN AIRPLANE	FESTIVAL OR CENCERT	AT A PARTY

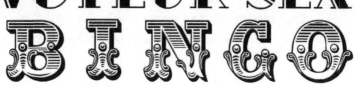

Spice Things Up

Here are a few helpful, handy tips for couples to consider. You can use just these tips to help spice up your sex life or integrate them into games. Above all, be creative, have fun and be safe.

Beyond the Bedroom

The first things that we'll talk about is not so much a game in and of itself, so much as a guideline. When it comes to all of the sex games listed here, don't be afraid to explore each others body's beyond the bedroom.

Most of these games can be adapted to be played in the shower, in the kitchen, in a hotel room, or even in your office if you're feeling a bit risqué. Sometimes the bedroom can feel a bit restrictive and something as simple as a change in environment can have a profound effect on the sex life for couples. As always, when playing any of these sex game, keep you mind open to new possibilities.

Dirty Talk

Guys, if you're going to come at me personally, you'd best be trained in the art of dirty talk.

The use of dirty talk cannot be emphasized enough here. Talking dirty to your spouse is the ultimate foreplay game. Not only will it let your lover know what you want them to do to you and what you want to do to them, talking dirty to your spouse will build up the sexual tension leading up to a climax in the bedroom.

The best part about dirty talk is that it can be done anywhere. Sending your spouse dirty text messages at work is a great way to build up anticipation for when you both get off of work and get off at home.

Dirty talk is also an important part of intercourse. Communication doesn't stop at the bedroom – during the act, your spouse will want you to open up and hear all of the things that turn you on.

Some people find that dirty talk is difficult for them, or they are embarrassed to talk dirty. Rest assure that with your loving spouse there is nothing to be embarrassed about.

If you are having trouble finding the right words to use, try easing into your dirty talk by simply describing things that you like to do in the bedroom.

Let your spouse know that you want to get better at dirty talk and have them help you ease your way into it. You'll find that dirty talk itself is one of the best sex games.

Massage Techniques

Giving and getting sensual massages with your partner is one of the most intimate a rewarding things the two of your can do together, but only if you actually enjoy the massage. There is nothing more unsexy than your spouse pushing on your back like they are tenderizing meat. Here are some basic massage techniques that will last you your entire marriage.

First, just as important as the massage itself is the atmosphere in which the massage takes place. Have you ever been to a massage spa? The will often be playing new age music and have scented candles scattered throughout the room. While you can skips the sounds of waterfalls and new age music, you might want to incorporate things like scented candles, incense and make sure that the room is in a warm temperature in order to set a romantic and comfortable atmosphere for your spouses massage.

Both the person giving the massage and the person receiving the massage should be in a relaxed mood prior to beginning. It helps to take a few deep breaths and focus on each individual muscle group and relaxing every muscle in your body. If you're receiving a massage, try not to tense up your muscles or you will not be able to enjoy the massage.

If you're giving the massage, start by warming the heat activated oils or lotion in your hands prior to touching your spouses back. Begin by spreading the oil on your hands all along the back of your spouse and feeling their different muscle groups as you do this. If these is an area on their back that will require specific attention, like a knot or extreme tension, you should be able to feel that immediately. Apply gentle pressure to each section of their back at first while you "feel it out" in order to find out what area will require any special attention.

Use long, languid strokes slowly up and down your spouses back. Avoid using hard downward pressure anywhere on their body. If you find a knot or tension on your spouse, use make small, gentle circles on that area until you can feel the pressure disperse. Focus some attention on you spouse's shoulders and neck, which are both areas where a lot of tension and knots tend to build up. Again, you can use small circles with your thumbs in these areas, but always be receptive to the amount of pressure that you are applying. Remember, this is supposed to be a sensual massage, not a deep tissue tenderizing. Try not to talk during the massage, which will reinforce the tranquility of the experience.

Make sure that you finish one area in entirety before you move on to another area. A good masseuse will also work the other person's arms, legs, head, and since this is a couple's massage, finish with the other person's genitals. Be gentle, be calm, take it slow, and keep it sensual.

Lastly, as with many aspects of sex in marriage, you will want to make sure that the other person gets a chance to get a massage. By now, they probably have a lot of build up tension throughout their body as well and will surely need to be relieved.

Don't forget the massage oil!

https://amzn.to/34zTVG5

Adult Films

Watching adult films together with your spouse is a fantastic way for you to bond and possibly broaden your sexual horizons. Even if the two of you have never been a fan of pornography before, you might find that you enjoy watching adult films together as a married couple.

Talk to your spouse about the idea and what you would like to get out of watching an adult film together. Are you just looking to get turned on, or are you looking for inspiration for a few new positions to try together? Whatever your reason, there are a wide variety of adult films that may challenge the ideas you have about pornography. They now make adult films specifically with couple in mind. There are adult films which emphasize the romantic and story aspects of the movie and even many "how-to" adult films that will walk you through trying out new and exciting positions. If you and you spouse have a very special thing that you enjoy in the bedroom, there is almost certainly an entire library of adult films on that subject.

On your next trip to your local adult toy store, browse the adult film section. Most sex stores have a very extensive library of adult films. Decide on one that you will both enjoy and commit to watching it together. You'll find that not only will you bond by watching adult movies together, you might see something that the two of you want to try together.

Any adult film can be made into a sex game for couples. The first time you watch a new adult film together, see if you can keep up with the actors in the movie. Every time the stars in the movie switch positions, you and your spouse switch to the same position. See if the two of you can act out the entire movie in every single position and achieve the stamina of a porn star. Whether you are actually able to accomplish this or not, you will both have a good time.

Ladies, this is a great ice-breaker to turn any conversation or situation sexual with a guy you like.

Fun Drawer

This is a must for every couple. On your nightstand, dresser, or in your closet if you have kids, set up a "fun drawer".

What is a fun drawer? A fun drawer is a designated drawer somewhere in your bedroom (it's best if it is within reach of your actual bed) that if full of sexy items. This can include condoms, lubricant, massage oils, blindfolds, handcuffs, dildos, whips, items that you use for your role playing fantasies or whatever you and your spouse enjoy in the bedroom.

Make sure that you fill your fun drawer with items that both you and your spouse can enjoy. The fun drawer should be an exciting idea that you can reference outside of the bedroom, teasing your spouse that "tonight he/she can choose something from the fun drawer to play with." As time passes and you get to know your spouse better, you will watch your fun drawer grow into the best, personalized collection of sex games for the two of you.

If you're looking for ideas on items that you can incorporate into your fun drawer at first, consider the basics. Ask yourself what you and your spouse both enjoy. Some natural choices you may want to include are condoms, lubricant, lotions, scented candles or incense, and anything else that will help you set the mood.

You should also talk to your spouse about incorporating novelty sex toys into your lovemaking. Start slow by going to a reputable adult novelty store and picking out one toy for her that she agrees to use the next time the two of you are in the bedroom.

Depending on how she enjoys your new toy you will have a better idea of what toy to get next. Most adult novelty stores also have a wide selection of sex toys for men as well.

Be open minded and honest with yourself and your lover about what items you will enjoy using in the bedroom. Remember that a sun drawer is supposed to be fun and that you should never stop growing and adding to it.

And for the record, to this date, no man has ever let me peg them ;-(

Your Sex Store and You

As couples begin to explore one another, as well as getting to know their own sexuality a little bit better, you will want to get comfortable with your local sex toy store.

All couples should make at least one trip to a sex store at some point during the course of their relationship. While couples may find that sex stores are not for them, most sex stores offer a wide variety of way for couples to explore their sexuality together while keeping their life in the bedroom fresh – all in a safe, comforting, and judgment-free atmosphere.

Whether you're a new couple or have been married for years, you should never be ashamed while seeking to explore each other's sexuality, and you should never be embarrassed to shop at a sex toy store.

Today, most sex toy store employees are nurturing, knowledgeable and take an interest in helping you find the right toys that work for your unique dynamic. If you find that this is not the case, you might want to look for a store that better suits your needs and desires. Try looking online for reviews of local sex stores in order to avoid going to the seedy, creepy ones. Usually, you can't go wrong with sex toy chain stores.

Once you find a sex toy store that you like, get to know the staff by name. Let them know that you just got married and are looking to explore your sexuality. By having an open, honest conversation with the employees, they will be able to make recommendations that best suit your needs. In order to make sure that there is never a dull moment in the bedroom, make a habit of visiting your favorite local sex toy store at least once a month.

You and your spouse can take turns picking our new items to introduce into the bedroom and new addition to your "fun drawer".

Don't be afraid to ask for help or be a little adventurous.

Sexy Toys for Couples: My Personal Recommendations

FOR HER

- **Hits all the right spots:**
  Classic Rabbit Vibrator for Women -
  https://amzn.to/3sFzLSW
- **Waterproof Kinky set:**
  6pcs Waterproof Silicone Anales Trainer Set Pleasure Plug Toys -
  https://amzn.to/3oO1Rds
- **Remote controlled fun:**
  Remote controlled clit stimulator vibratior -
  https://amzn.to/3uQT2mZ
- **For "alone time":**
  Vibrating Didlo for Women -
  https://amzn.to/3oLI4vq

FOR HIM

- **Classic cock ring:**
  Soft silicone cock ring for men - https://amzn.to/3BAbRwl
- **Guys with a little kink:**
  Cockring for For Sex Men Vibrant Pennis Ring Prostate Massager - https://amzn.to/3BlyVOW
- **Guys solo play:**
  Male heated masturabator Pleasure Toys - https://amzn.to/3sIlsgd

HIM OR HER

- **The unbeatable classic:**
  Hitatchi Magic Wand personal massager - https://amzn.to/3uRgOiD
- **The holy grail:**
  G-spot vibrator for men and women - https://amzn.to/3sJQynV
- **For tingling electric sensations:**
  TENS 7000 Digital TENS Unit with Accessories - https://amzn.to/3rOjP1m

Even More Sexy, Dirty, Kinky, Naughty & Raunch-tastic Games for Couples

As you've already seen throughout the course of this book, you don't need to spend any money to bond with your partner in the bedroom over some fun and sexy games. That being said, some of you adventurous couples out there will probably burn through most or all of the games in this book fairly quickly, and if you're married, "'til death do us part" can be a long fucking time (excuse my filthy mouth).

That's why I've compiled a list of my personal favorite and highly recommended fun & flirty, down & dirty games on Amazon that couples can play together. I've personally spent a ton of money on games such as these and let me tell you - there are a lot of duds out there! So, in the interest of saving you and your beau the time and money involved in sorting through the bullshit games to get to the good ones, please enjoy this list of my personal sexy game recommendations.

1. The Discovery Adult Game for Couples - Date Night in a Box - https://amzn.to/3oOm5nv
2. Pillow Talkn 100 Date Night Ideas Cards - https://amzn.to/3BjCLIF
3. Talk, Flirt, Dare! Fun and Romantic Game for Couples: Https://amzn.to/3uQUNkg
4. Dare Duel - A Romantic Game for Couples - https://amzn.to/3JuuCUE
5. Adult Sexy Time Spinner Game for Couples - https://amzn.to/3JsMsaj
6. WHY DON'T WE Spice it Up Romantic and Fun Card Game for Couples - https://amzn.to/34zUfVj
7. Couples Connection Cards: for Date Nights, Deep Conversation, Intimacy, Relationships, One on One and Romance - https://amzn.to/3LAs355
8. Favors Box Sexy Coupon Categories for Couples – https://amzn.to/3JrmQup
9. Dirty Minds Card Game - https://amzn.to/3Jz77d7
10. Intimacy: Romance in a Box - https://amzn.to/3oPBpAe

Parting Words

Who says that once the ring goes on, couples should pry their hands away from one another?

If we have learned anything in the 2022 edition of this book, it's that happy relationships can take many different forms.

- ✓ Married.
- ✓ Committed.
- ✓ Monogamous.
- ✓ Open.
- ✓ Swinging.
- ✓ Thruple.
- ✓ Exclusive and/or non-exclusive fuck buddy.
- ✓ Friends with benefits.
- ✓ Enemies with benefits (read: hate fuck)

Although it's generally the committed relationships that give couples an opportunity to let themselves feel truly sexually uninhibited, trust will always be the deciding factor when it comes to who is ready and willing to get freaky with you.

For married couples, it can sometimes seem difficult to keep the spark (in between your legs, that is) alive. When this happens, take it as an opportunity to experiment, try out a few new things, and continue searching for fresh things that you can experience together. This is, after all, the person whom you will be spending the rest of your life with, who just agreed to love you until death do you part, so feel free to cut loose with your spouse and let them know all of your dirtiest, sexiest fantasies and desires. After getting hitched, you should feel free to divulge all of your wants and desires to the person you just married, because if you can't tell your spouse, who can you tell?

When all is said and done and you finally begin to catch your breath, sex games are not just about having a great time in bed. Sex games are about bringing couples together and bonding in the most intimate way imaginable. It's about building that trust.

After all, when things are going well for two people in the bedroom, everything else in life seems to be going well, also. Once you and your spouse are able to connect on an intimate, physical level, having open emotional communication will become easier. As will most things in your relationship.

Through the use of the sex games for couples provided in this book, I hope that I have brought you and your partner a little closer in your relationship and in the bedroom.

And, guys, I also hope that this book has inspired you to work a little harder in the bedroom. Seriously, start putting in a little more effort, and we women will notice and reward it handsomely.

Years from now, you sex life with your partner may be every stronger, hotter, and more passionate than what it is today. In any relationship, just as in life, you should never lose sight of that passion, just as you should never lose that same primal attraction that you feel towards your partner.

See you in the next edition of Sexy, Dirty, Naughty Games for Couples.

- XOXO,
  Allison Eden

The Index of Kinks

Kinks for Inanimate Objects

Agalmatophilia - a sexual attraction for human-like statues, dolls, mannequins. This differs from Pygmalionism, which refers to an attraction to items of one's own creation.

Altocalciphilia - sexually turned on by high heels, usually worn by women but not always.

Balloons Fetish - sexual arousal from balloons which often involves inflation of one's body part by inserting balloons underneath clothes.

Belonephilia - sexual arousal to sharp items, such as needles, pins, razors.

Corsetry - wearing a corset to change one's body shape.

Diaper Fetish - sexual arousal from diapers and/or the use of it. It is usually incorporated into infantilism, scat, watersports, humiliation, and dominance.

Fire Play - any sexual practice involving fire.

Food Play - any sexual practice involving food. This may mean using someone as a dish or table, covering your partner's body with food and licking it off (think whipped cream or chocolate sauce, but you can get creative!).

Keraunophilia - sexual arousal from thunder and lightning.

Kigurumi - a sexual attraction to the wearing of a cosplay costume or anime mask.

Knife Play - a practice of running a knife or a blade along your partner to enhance sexual gratification.

Latex/rubber Fetish - sexual preference for latex, rubber, PVC and similar materials.

Mechanophilia - a sexual attraction to machines and/or doing sex act in/on a certain type of a machine, such as cars, washing machines, androids and etc.

Pygmalionism - sexual attachment with a human-like creation of one's own work, e.g. rubbing oneself against a statue.

Plushophilia - a sexual attraction to stuffed animals or soft toys. In order to have sexual interactions with their toys, people modify their plushies with a hole or holes.

Retifism - sexual arousal to shoes or other footwear.

Robotism - sexual arousal to robots, aroused by using a robot in a sex act.

Ropework - a sexual obsession with rope, especially in the context of bondage in BDSM.

Siderodromophilia - sexual arousal to trains or riding in trains.

Stigmatophilia - sexually aroused by piercings and tattoos, especially in genitals and/or nipples.

Stockings - sexual arousal to the wearing of stockings.

Strap-on - sexual arousal to wearing strap-on for anal, oral or vaginal penetration.

Technophilia - a sexual attraction to technology, such as cyborgs, robots, mechas and sex machines.

Tentacles - a sexual obsession with tentacles which is usually a fictional creature and depicted in porn or erotic animation.

Thesauromania - a sexual obsession with a collection of women clothing, especially underwear.

Underwear - a sexual obsession with underwear which usually involves a man who likes to smell, wear or collect women's underwear.

Uniforms - sexually aroused by seeing your partner wearing a certain type of uniform.

Wax play - a form of temperature play in BDSM which applies wax to stimulate a slight burning sensation to the skin.

Weapon fetish - sexual arousal to weapons.

Wet and messy (WAM) fetish - sexually aroused by the act of applying wet, slime and messy substances other than bodily fluids to the naked skin or clothes. Also known as sploshing.

Xylophilia - sexual arousal to wood.

Yeastiality - sexual arousal to baked food which has risen with yeast, such as bread, pastry, and especially warm dough. People with this obsession are also attracted by partners with yeast infection as applying yeast to the genitals can lead to an infection.

Kinks for Non-Humans

Dendrophilia - sexually attracted to trees.

Formicophilia - sexually turned on by being crawling upon or nibbled by insects, such as ants, cockroaches, etc.

Zoophilia - sexual arousal or sexual preference for non-human animals. It is **NOT** the actual act of having sex with animals. Only having erotic feelings or fantasies involving animals is not against the law.

Kinks for Body Parts

Acomoclitic - a sexual attraction to hairless genitals.

Armpits Fetish - sexual arousal from smelling, licking, or kissing armpits.

Cock and/or ball Fetish - a sexual obsession with cocks and balls.

Foot Fetish - a sexual obsession with the foot.

Macrogenitalism - a sexual attraction to huge genitals.

Nasolingus - sexual arousal to licking and/or sucking someone's nose.

Nasophilia - sexual arousal to noses.

Oculolinctus - sexual arousal from licking eyeballs.

Oculophilia - sexual arousal to eyes.

Odontophilia - a sexual obsession with teeth, e.g. licking your partner's teeth or biting them with your teeth.

Partialism - a sexual obsession for a specific part of the body, such as feet, breasts, hair and etc.

Quirofilia - sexual arousal to hands. It could be an obsession with a certain shape of hands, or part of hands, such as fingers, fingernails, or simply doing a certain action with hands, e.g. washing dishes with hands.

Trichophilia - a sexual obsession with human hair, most commonly head hair, people with this kink or fetish get arousal from viewing, touching or in some extreme cases eating hair.

Kinks for Bodily Waste

Golden Showers - any sex act involving urine, it is also known as " watersports"

Hematolagnia - sexual arousal from blood, it usually involves drinking, licking, looking at blood through bloodletting or biting.

Menophilia - sexual arousal from menstrual blood.

Mysophilia - sexually turned on by smelling or tasting items soiled with human fluids during sex, such as an undergarment or used tampon.

Olfactophilia - sexual arousal by smells and odors emanating from the body, especially the sexual area.

Scatophilia -sexual arousal to feces, it is also called "coprophilia".

Vomit - sexual arousal from vomiting or substance of vomit.

Kinks for Specific Partners

Allorgasmia - sexual arousal from fantasizing about having sex with someone else other than your current partner.

Anonymous Sex - a practice of having sex with someone that you are not aware of his/her identity, e.g. glory hole.

Gerontophilia - sexual preference for the elderly.

Hybristophilia - a sexual attraction to someone who is known to have "committed an outrage or crime, such as rape, murder, or armed robbery." In some cases, the person who is the focus of sexual desire is someone who has been imprisoned. In some cases, the hybristophilia may urge and coerce their partner to commit a crime.

Macro Fetish - a sexual attraction to beings larger than themselves in the context of sexual fantasy, e.g. a man with Marco fetish would be aroused by the fantasy of being abused, degraded or eaten by a giantess.

Maiesiophilia - sexually turned on by pregnant women or the act of giving birth.

Micro Fetish -a sexual attraction to being small or doing the sex act with small partners.

Morphophilia - a sexual attraction to partners with a certain type of body characteristics (e.g., shape, size, skin and hair color) that are different from one's own, such as fat people, amputees and dwarves.

Parthenophilia - sexual preference for virgins, especially girls with delayed puberty. **Fantasy is ok, the actual act may constitute a crime!**

Savantophilia - sexual arousal to people who are cognitively impaired or developmentally delayed.

Somnophilia - sexual fascination with sleeping or unconscious individual. Also known as "sleeping beauty syndrome".

Teratophilia - a sexual attraction to monsters or deformed people.

Xenophilia - a sexual attraction to that which is unknown or different from one's native experiences, e.g. a sexual desire for aliens and mutants.

Kinks for Specific Settings

Acrophilia - sexually excited by heights, or doing sex act at great heights.

Actirasty - sexual arousal from sun exposure. It is often associated with sexual arousal to engaging in sexual activities outdoors.

Agoraphilia - preference for having sex in public places or outdoors, it is illegal to practice in most parts of the world.

Aquaphilia - a sexual attraction to water, places with water and activities under water.

Claustrophilia - sexually aroused by confinement in small, enclosed spaces.

Imprisonment - sexual arousal from being confined to a certain area or place, such as a cage.

Intoxication - sexual preference for taking drugs or drinking alcohol before or during a sex act.

Nyctophilia - sexual preference for being in the dark or night.

Psychrophilia - a sexual obsession with the cold or watching someone being frozen.

Telephonicophilia - sexual arousal from talking about sexual and erotic matters over the phone.

Kinks for Physical Pain

Acrotomophilia - sexually aroused by amputees (legs or arms).

Apotemnophilia - sexual arousal from having your own limbs amputated.

Castration - sexually aroused by removal of male testicles, in fact, it is an extremely dangerous practice, most likely it is only the thought or fantasy of castration arouses people.

Feederism - sexual arousal from feeding oneself or another with the intention of gaining weight or increasing body size.

Masochism - physically or psychologically suffering pain or humiliation for sexual gratification.

Needle Play - sexually turned on by piercing, scratching the skin with needles.

Nullification - sexually turned on by removal of a body part.

Nullo - sexually turned on by removal of genitals.

Odaxelagnia - sexually aroused by biting or being bitten.

Sadism - sexual arousal from inflicting physical or psychological pain and/or humiliation on others.

Symphorphilia - sexual arousal from watching car accidents or other traumatic incidents.

Urtication - a practice of applying stinging nettles to stimulate the skin for sexual gratification.

Vaccinophilia - sexually aroused by getting vaccinated.

Kinks for Role Play Scenario

Age play - a form of roleplay between adults in which both parties act in different ages, e.g. infantilism, Daddy/daughter play.

Aliens - a fantasy about having sex with aliens which often happens in an abduction or forced scenario.

Impregnation - sexually turned on by the possibility of getting pregnant during unprotected vaginal intercourse for both parties.

Infantilism - a form of roleplay in which one participant acts like an infant or baby, the other one plays a parental role.

Medical Play - a medical-themed roleplay in which sexual partners use medical equipment and wear uniforms to take on relevant roles in that scenario.

Pet Play - a kink in which one person dresses and acts like a pet.

Pony Play - a kink for dressing up and acting like a pony.

Puppy Play - a type of roleplay in which one takes on the role of a puppy.

Harpaxophilia - sexual arousal from being the victim of a robbery.

Phygephilia - a sexual thrill from being a fugitive on the run.

Vampire - sexual fascination with a vampire or role-play of a vampire.

Kinks for Specific Sex Acts

Anal Sex - a practice of inserting penis, fingers, or sex toys into the anus for sexual pleasure.

Enemas - a practice of injecting fluid into the rectum to empty bowel. It is also used in preparation for anal play.

Pegging - woman-on-man anal sex in which a woman penetrates a male with a strap-on.

Rimming - an oral-to-anal sexual practice in which one person stimulates another person by licking, kissing, sucking their anus.

Barebacking - having sex without wearing a condom. Note that, it is dangerous as it will lead to STI transmission or pregnancy.

Body Painting - sexual arousal to the act of painting bodies.

Clothed Sex - sexual preference for having sex with clothes on,

Cross-dressing - dressing like your opposite gender which involves clothing, accessories, makeup, and wigs.

Crush fetish - sexual arousal to the act of crushing, it typically involves watching or performing the crushing of small insects, animals or food.

Dacryphilia - sexual arousal to seeing tears or crying.

Double Penetration - penetration of a woman's vagina and anus by penises or sex toys at the same time.

Figging - inserting a peeled ginger root into someone's anus or vagina to generate a burning sensation.

Fisting - penetrating a hand into a virginal or ass.

Impact Play - a form of BDSM practice in which one hits another for sexual pleasure, such as spanking.

Caning - beating someone with a cane to get sexual pleasure.

Flogging - hitting someone with particular implements such as lashes, whips, switches, rods, etc..

Spanking - sexually aroused by spanking or being spanked. The act of spanking is usually done with your bare hands, whips, paddles or other implements.

Internal Cumshots - a sex act of ejaculating into a female's vagina.

Intercrural or Interfemoral Sex - thrusting between someone's thighs without penetration.

Lactation - sexual pleasure from breastfeeding, it could be watching women lactate, sucking on women's milk-filled breasts and/or having sex with lactating women.

Pictophilia - sexual arousal to watching porn, especially of the same act or actor.

Revving - sexual arousal from seeing someone (usually a female) rev an engine, especially when they wear stockings or high-heels. Also known as "car cranking" or "pedal pumping."

Sensation Play - a practice of stimulating body senses to heighten sexual gratification, it usually includes the use of silk scarves, feathers, ice, massage oils, and other similar implements. Unlike BDSM play which is about suffering and power exchange, sensation play is pleasing and light for both vanilla and kinksters.

Knismolagnia - sexually aroused by tickling or being tickled as it will trigger some of the same muscles as orgasms.

Zentai - sexual preference for wearing skin-tight suits that cover you from head to toe in a sex act. People with this preference get aroused by the feeling of being anonymous and/or the hugging sensation of being in tight suits.

Sensory Deprivation - sex act that removes or reduces body senses, e.g. blindfolds used for blocking eyesight.

Blindfolds - sexual preference for wearing a blindfold when having sex.

Pecattiphilia - sexual arousal from doing something considered sinful by your religion, e.g. any conduct of the seven deadly sins.

Kinks for Restriction

Amaurophilia - sexual preference for not being able to see during sex, i.e. turning off the lights or blindfolding a partner.

Bondage - restraining someone or tying them up to arouse sexual gratification for both parties.

Breath play - a practice of limiting breath for sexual gratification.

Choking - restricting one's breathing and blood supply to the brain by applying pressure to the carotid arteries with hands, a scarf, or a chokehold.

Gags - a device that is put over or in somebody's mouth to stop them speaking. Gags are usually associated with role plays involving bondage, but that is not necessarily the case.

Hypoxia - a rare form of autoerotic asphyxiation in which a person gets aroused by the effect of oxygen deprivation when being submerged under water. This can be fatal.

Japanese Bondage - a form of bondage originated in Japan. It is called "Kinbaku" in Japanese, the term "Kin" means "tight" and "baku" means "restraint". Unlike western bondage, it is not only for the purpose of erotic pleasure; it is more of a type of art.

Mummification - a specific type of bondage in which one participant is completely or partially wrapped in materials such as a plastic wrap, bondage tape, duct tape, etc., but it can be dangerous if bindings prevent airflow.

Orgasm Control - a sexual practice of taking control over how, when and if an orgasm will take place.

Orgasm Denial - a sexual practice in which one person is kept at a high level of sexual arousal for an extended period of time without orgasm.

Kinks for Power Exchange

Begging - begging to have sex or organism.

Collaring - wearing a collar or seeing others being collared to show submission to a dominant.

Discipline - a practice of training a submissive to be obedient to a dominant, punishment inflicted for a defined infraction.

Kinks for Humiliation

Cuckolding - a sexual obsession in which a man gets aroused by watching his female partner having sex with other men.

Degradation - a practice of sexual humiliation or abuse for gratification.

Dirty Talk - using explicit and arousing words to talk about sexual activity.

Face Sitting - a sex act whereby one person sits on another person's face for pleasure, both parties could be anyone of any gender identity or sexuality.

Face Slapping - sexually turned on by slapping someone's face or being face-slapped.

Penis Humiliation - a kink involving insulting a man's penis, including size, appearance, and performance.

Queening - a sex act in which a woman sits on her partner's face for pleasure.

Kinks for Exposing/ Being Exposed

Agrexophilia - sexually aroused by having other people know about your sexual activities. This includes having sex in public places, playing your sex video online, or bragging about your conquests.

Exhibitionism - sexual preference for having sex or being naked in front of other people. **Be careful, this could be illegal!**

Katoptronophilia - sexual arousal from doing a sexual activity in front of a mirror, such as having sex, masturbating and etc.

Mixophilia - sexual arousal from watching others (with their consent and knowledge) or yourself doing sex act, e.g. having sex in front of a mirror.

Voyeurism - sexual arousal from spying on people being naked or engaged in sexual activities. Non-consensual voyeurism may be against the law.

Vicarphilia - sexual arousal from hearing narratives about other people's (sexual) activities, experiences and behaviors.

Kinks for Multiple Partners

Group Sex - a sexual activity which involves more than two participants. It occurs between people of all sexual orientations and genders.

Polyiterophilia - sexual preference for group sex.

Triolism - sexual arousal to threesomes. This may include watching your partner have sex with someone else.

Kinks for sexual orientation

Andromimetophilia - a sexual attraction to females who dress or act like men, or female-to-male transsexuals.

Autoandrophilia - a biological female gets aroused by the idea of becoming a male.

Lesbophilia - a fetishistic fascination (typically in non-lesbians) with lesbians and erotic contact between women.

Yaoi - sexual arousal to male-on-male sexuality in anime, manga, or fan fiction. Aimed at a female audience, not a gay male.

The Forbidden Fetishes

Bestiality - the act of having sex with non-human animals.

Hybristophilia - behaviors involving sexual activity with someone who is known to have "committed an outrage or crime, such as rape, murder, or armed robbery."

Necrophilia - behaviors involving sexual activity with human corpses.

Necrozoophilia - the act of killing animals in order to have sex with their dead bodies.

Pedophilia - behaviors involving sexual activity with a prepubescent child or children - generally age 13 years or younger.

Raptophilia - the act of committing rape in order to get sexual gratification, it is also called "biastophilia".

Snuff - the act of killing or being killed for sexual gratification. It is believed that it is only an urban legend, but there are films about real people being tortured and killed on the internet which is extremely brutal and illegal in practice.

Vore/Vorarephilia - the act of eating someone while they are still alive or being eaten in order to get sexual gratification. It is incredibly dangerous and illegal in practice.

About the Author

Writing is therapeutic for Allison Eden, who channels her daddy issues into her erotic romance novels (Coming Soon!). A voyeur, sub, and a bit of a nudist, Allison does her best writing while sitting by the bay windows in her birthday suit.

Recommended Reading

Although they admittedly have absolutely nothing to do with sex, here are some other books you might enjoy from Words Are Swords Publishing.

Free on Kindle Unlimited

Learn to Conquer Any Fear, Phobia, or Anxiety in Under 60-Minutes

Steven Matthews

This book explains the fundamental strategy that people around the world use to conquer their fears and phobias permanently! Even the most stubborn of irrational phobias can be conquered, thereby lowering your stress levels and dramatically improving your health. All it takes is 60 minutes of your time. What have you got to lose?

https://amzn.to/32ETPsk

YOUR CLOTHES ARE KILLING YOU! The Little -Known Fact About How Some Fabrics Heal & Some Can Kill

Steven Matthews

This book is a deep dive into the fascinating world of fabrics, and if "fascinating fabrics" sounds like an oxymoron to you, then just try and say that after reading this book! You don't have to be a seamstress, sewing machine junkie, or even a fan of fashion to benefit from this book, and who knows? It may even save your life.

https://amzn.to/32LsPYd

The Laws of Persuasion, Manipulation & Influence

Steven Matthews

This book will help you to better understand these laws and gives situational examples of how they can be used to influence others. You will also learn the principles of influence in dark persuasion psychology that are proven to work on the human brain.

https://amzn.to/38NgqHf

Homestead Business Secrets to Living a Sustainable Life

Steven Matthews

Homestead Secrets is the perfect book for dreamers who are still weighing the options of starting a homestead and homestead beginners who are just starting out, as well as intermediate homesteaders who just need a few more good ideas on how to make money homesteading or marketing the products and services they currently produce on the homestead.

https://amzn.to/3nn46kP

Everything but the Wood Tiny House Essential Information + Free Tiny House Building Blueprints & Floor Plans

Steven Matthews

The author understands that building your first Tiny House can be scary! Rest assured that all of the tools in this one book will arm you with the knowledge and confidence you need to build a tiny home that will be an endless source of adventure for generations to come - No experience necessary!

https://amzn.to/36DN9Ma

101 Marijuana Horticulture Secrets

Steven Matthews

This book was written to help beginner and intermediate growers with common problems which all cannabis growers will experience eventually. These are the tried-and-true experiences of a veteran grower who speaks from experience. Everything contained in 101 Marijuana Horticulture Secrets is 100% real and advice you can count on.

https://amzn.to/2IPLDyJ

Perfection is a Lie: A Weight-Positive Book of Body Acceptance, Self-Esteem & Confidence

Steven Matthews

Perferction is a Lie is the body-positive book that understands what teenagers are going through will help walk them through building healthy expectations when it comes to self-acceptance, self-esteem and self-image.

https://amzn.to/3msNfxH

Bestselling Business Books

Become a master of modern day business-building techniques, highly-effective sales tactics, & the most up-to-date marketing trends with all 4 books in the *Brand & Business Applied Marketing Strategies* series.

With practical and effective marketing strategies designed for **personal brands**, **ecommerce businesses, product merchants** and **service providers** in any industry, each book in the 4 part Brand and Business Applied Marketing Strategies series covers an essential part of building a profitable business.

Packed with **bonus content, free tools,** and **downloadable resources**, each book in the series features an **interactive workbook, business planner,** and **expertly crafted guide** designed to take personal brands & businesses on a **growth-to-scale** journey.

The advanced marketing strategies included in each planner and workbook were meticulously written with the end goal of creating a **sustainable** and **profitable** business that can be built for **longevity** in any industry.

3 Days to Launch, 1,000 Days to Mastery: The 2022 Business & Personal Branding Workbook & Planner

This step-by-step guide for both business & personal brands will take you on an expertly guided journey from the essentials of launching a profitable brand in just 3 days, to building a business that is adored by customers and coveted by industry peers. The Branding Planner and Workbook includes new Action Items each day to guarantee an upward trajectory of steady growth.

+BONUS CONTENT includes dozens of time-saving templates & free business tools designed to help brands build faster, find more customers, and out perform the competition. ($10,000+ Value!)

The 2022 Growth Hacking SEO Workbook & Planner

The latest digital marketing workbook and SEO planner for personal brands and businesses who want to growth-hack WordPress, WooCommerce, keyword targeting strategies and more. Includes the most up-to-date on-page & off-page SEO marketing strategies for INSANE Traffic & Growth.

+BONUS CONTENT includes access to hundreds of free web building tools, growth-hacking journal, industry-specific keyword strategies & more. ($8,500+ Value!)

Influencer Growth Hacking: The 2022 Social Media Marketing Strategies Calendar & Workbook

Plan your rise to fame, fandom, and profitability with the *2020 Influencer Growth Hacking* calendar that tells you exactly when and how to use advanced social media marketing strategies. The Social Media Marketing

Workbook helps influencer, personal brands, and businesses track, improve, and scale up their engagement and overall social reach.

+BONUS CONTENT includes free social media marketing tools to help influencers rapidly optimize engagement, track effective campaigns & build authority in any industry. ($2,500 Value!)

Low Bids, Big Results: The 2022 Advertising Strategies & Copywriting Workbook

Start getting the most out of your pay-per-click ad campaigns with highly effective PPC bidding strategies, audience-dependent copywriting techniques, finding often-overlooked keywords, and low CPC / high conversion rate advertising templates for Google, Facebook, Amazon, YouTube, Bing, forums & more.

+BONUSES include hundreds of dollars in free ad credits for Google AdWords, Microsoft Bing, Facebook Business, Amazon AMS & More!